HAL•LEONARD
INSTRUMENTAL
PLAY-ALONG

AUDIO
ACCESS
INCLUDED

PLAYBACK+
Speed • Pitch • Balance • Loop

ALTO SAX

Disney

THE

LION KING

T0079100

Audio arrangements by Peter Deneff

To access audio visit:
www.halleonard.com/mylibrary

Enter Code
2813-1726-6003-3069

Motion Picture Artwork TM & Copyright © 2019 Disney

ISBN 978-1-5400-6568-1

HAL•LEONARD®

Visit Hal Leonard Online at
www.halleonard.com

Contact us:
Hal Leonard
7777 West Bluemound Road
Milwaukee, WI 53213
Email: info@halleonard.com

In Europe, contact:
Hal Leonard Europe Limited
42 Wigmore Street
Marylebone, London, W1U 2RN
Email: info@halleonardeurope.com

In Australia, contact:
Hal Leonard Australia Pty. Ltd.
4 Lentara Court
Cheltenham, Victoria, 3192 Australia
Email: info@halleonard.com.au

CONTENTS

CAN YOU FEEL THE LOVE TONIGHT

ALTO SAX

Music by ELTON JOHN
Lyrics by TIM RICE

CIRCLE OF LIFE

ALTO SAX

Music by ELTON JOHN
Lyrics by TIM RICE

HAKUNA MATATA

ALTO SAX

Music by ELTON JOHN
Lyrics by TIM RICE

I JUST CAN'T WAIT TO BE KING

ALTO SAX

Music by ELTON JOHN
Lyrics by TIM RICE

8

HE LIVES IN YOU

ALTO SAX

Music and Lyrics by MARK MANCINA,
JAY RIFKIN and LEBOHANG MORAKE

THE LION SLEEPS TONIGHT

ALTO SAX

New Lyrics and Revised Music by GEORGE DAVID WEISS,
HUGO PERETTI and LUIGI CREATORE

NEVER TOO LATE

ALTO SAX

Music by ELTON JOHN
Lyrics by TIM RICE

STAMPEDE

ALTO SAX

Composed by HANS ZIMMER

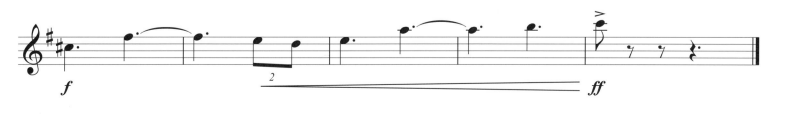

SPIRIT

ALTO SAX

Written by TIMOTHY McKENZIE,
ILYA SALMANZADEH and BEYONCÉ